Losing Purchase

poems by
Bruce Dethlefsen

Apprentice
House Press
Loyola University Maryland

First Edition

Library of Congress Control Number: 2022949968

Paperback ISBN: 978-1-62720-439-2
Ebook ISBN: 978-1-62720-440-8

Design by Mary Velazquez
Editorial Development by Corrine Moulds
Promotional Development by Shanley Honarvar

Published by Apprentice House Press

Apprentice
House Press
Loyola University Maryland

Loyola University Maryland
4501 N. Charles Street, Baltimore, MD 21210
410.617.5265
www.ApprenticeHouse.com
info@ApprenticeHouse.com

Who but Bruce Dethlefsen, poet extraordinaire, would claim confidently that every red-wing blackbird knows precisely whose cattail is whose—and that "the moon of the burning cold" always rises in "Januember"? Dethlefsen is widely known for never allowing a single shred of nuanced humor (as well as the knee-slapping kind) to slip away unnoticed—while simultaneously reminding us to "tighten up the spaces between us." Even his lightest poems convey an awareness of "how swift the nighthawk / flies above the hospice" – for which the reader is grateful. This latest collection, titled Losing Purchase, comes well-equipped with such wisdom, along with his customary openheartedness and joy.

— Marilyn L. Taylor, former Wisconsin Poet Laureate

What makes Dethlefsen's poems so touching is his willingness to be fully human—by turns goofy, curious, smitten, irreverent, helpless and hopeless. Here we find the poet as outdoorsman, as class clown, as devoted son, as humble teacher and (most movingly) as bereaved father. Through it all runs the sane wisdom of a survivor, for whom "the world is best taken in at walking speed."

—David Southward, author of *Bachelor Buttons*

Bruce Dethlefsen's poems surprise—a thunderstorm is really a catalog of evil, what could be a difficult childhood memory resounds with humor, and a poem that begins remembering his son's first steps and diapered-bottom baby dance shows how grief lives and moves. Losing Purchase is alive with mothers, mothers who laugh at you and with you, and mothers who epitomize loss. You'll find here kindness and care delivered in a deadpan voice amidst forest green. The poems themselves are full of a quiet urging—like a script the football coach taped next to the phone: pause for response / say thank you very much / say I love you mom dad or name of guardian." It's important, you see, because in the title poem Dethlefsen walks out on some shaky ice after both his sons have died and tells us "there are two sides to the ice / one upside and one down / one bright and sunny warm / one dark and most coldblooded /funny how there are people here you love / and then there aren't."

> — C. Kubasta, author of *Abjectification* and *Of Covenants*

*Thank you to the publications that have included
some of these poems.*

*A special thanks to Cathryn Cofell and Karla Huston,
my poetry sisters, for their poetic suggestions and encouragement,
and a nod to Sue Rose Allen for proofreading and the cover photo..*

in memory of my sons
Nathan and Willi

Contents

if rain

Day to Lean On

this is the day to lean on
make a breath to learn which names
these birds and trees call themselves
what it means to be that black
what it means to be so green
take the time the crows and pines
have entrusted you could spend
rest your softest eyes on them
the sky will never
be this blue again

New Moons

januember
the moon of the burning cold
farch
the slice of ice moon
mabruary
the peeking moon
aptember
the moon of potential
member
the reunion moon
joctober
the moon of dance and play
julust
the moon most beautiful
augril
the angry dog moon
senuary
what was that feeling moon
ouly
the two-faced moon
novay
moon of the closing door
and dune
the wall at the end of the world moon

October Clouds of Door County

these are festering old testament
born of cold water black
at the door of death clouds
visigoth and viking clouds
serious coffins of badger claws
towers forged in iron white oak
chainmail chainsaw steel wool
hammer and anvil clouds
that grind and scour the peninsula
pillage plow and plunder
dreadnaughts and drones
pirates and absentee landlords
robots and clones
a villainy of nimrods
accumulation of insider traitors
outlaws ace of spades grave robbers
marauders pharmaceutical reps
corporate and oakland raiders
theocrats berserkers plutocrats
call each cloud by its ancient name
tweed desalvo ditka butkus
quantrill thatcher borden arbuckle
pol pot pilate shaka zulu
chivington reagan mccarthy
hitler milosovich nixon walker trump
mothers hide your children
the clouds of october continue to come
they are no friend of this trembling earth
nor can they ever be trusted

If Rain

...and when the earth shall claim your limbs, then shall you truly dance. —Kahlil Gibran, The Prophet

for a second my son trusted me
he let go of the coffee table
long enough to grab hold
his toddler hands around my index fingers
I sang our favorite song
I feel good   boodum boodum boodum boo
I knew that I would   boodum boodum boodum boo
he stutter stepped then bent his knees to bounce
his james brown diapered bottom up and down

he held on tight but always fell
I always helped him up
my love can do me no harm
and we felt good

he learned to let go longer
to walk   to run   to dance
to ride a bike   then motorcycle
(as it turns out not well enough)

outside the hospital
a willow sways in the wind
the wind that pushes the clouds
the clouds that make the rain
the rain that fills the blue green lake
where the willow dances
I think if rain were a tree

it would be a willow
and all us trees   roots and limbs
we'd dance like everything

cardinals purple brown
down the setting sunflower
seeds at the feeder

Fairy Ring

last night's rain has gone and left
a perfect ring of brown button mushrooms
smack in the middle of our backyard lawn
a stamp cancelled by an unknown hand
in some screen-doored wisconsin post office
on an envelope addressed in pencil
and mailed around a million years ago
to announce the birth of baby greta
to comfort the henderson family's grief
to ted who went slug-nutty in the argonne
containing one folded white lace hankie
for your fourth grade teacher mrs jenkins
mom's old recipe for slumgullion
a donation for church basement coffee
a fairy ring   a crown as faint as northern spring
a reminder to circle the wagons
and tighten up the spaces between us

Song of Ennis Lake

the boyhood home of John Muir

rise up early
walk the path around the lake
plant one foot and then the other
quiet yourself
listen to the song   the silence

the morning shush of white pine needles
the red-winged blackbird announces
whose cattail is whose
the drumming stomp of the grouse on the hollow log
the fog burns off
the dragonfly flutters
the honey bees sizzle on the wild purple bergamot
the hummingbirds buzz the yellow foxglove
the sun sparkles on the water then silence
your foot snaps a twig
a raft of mallards quack
the squawk of sandhill cranes
goose heads bob up and down
the bear claws sharpen on the hickory
the antlers scrape the oak
the muskrat dives beneath the bank
the beaver drags a sapling in its wake
the swoop and splash of the eagle
the swoosh of the kingfisher
the tapping stops
the woodpecker bounces in its flight

bluegills pop at water bugs in the shallows

as the sun slides west around the sky
the shadows swirl and change
the sun declines to red and gold
the shadows grow
at moonrise the northern pike skirts through the minnows
the black bass boils the lily pad
the white-footed mouse looks that way and that
the little brown bat picks off mosquitoes
the crickets tell the temperature is falling
the bullfrog tunes the tympani

then darkness
the nighthawk wheezes overhead
the coyotes yip and whine around the fresh kill
the great horned owl swivels its head and stares
the endless rise and fall of the whippoorwill
heat lightning bursts behind a cloud
distant thunder rolls
the light rain on the marsh marigolds

you walk
you know to slow yourself
let go
slow down to hear the song exactly as it's sung
the melody and harmony
the tempo and the tone
this song is never sung the same way twice

you remember now
the world is best taken in at walking speed

it's in the silence you learn the song
and you learn the song by heart

Before the Rain

swallows sway on telephone lines
all faced the same direction
grazing cows lay down in meadows
aligned for their protection
poets lean way back in chairs
window gazing on perfection

Perfect Wisconsin

these clean clear water
these trees these hills
these clear clean air
these wind these snow
these stars in night
these leaves these petals perfect

those black people white
those brown people red and yellow
those gold people silver perfect

that unions busted
that sexual abuse
that guns all that guns
that prisons perfect

perfect wisconsin
just perfect

Harbinger

heavy wet
march snow
I scrape
the shovel thin
gravel path
to the mailbox
sandhill cranes
squawking

storm clouds hang
dark as a poet's clothesline
I clench my collar

Our Home

this time it's wisconsin
where the yellow sun
of a turn called morning
shines on the green cornfield
where the white pelican circles
to land on the blue lake
around evening
this time it's wisconsin
this patch of earth
will be our home forever
unless until
there's another storm come through
or we manage somehow
to wreck the whole cosmic joint again
this time it's wisconsin

three mothers

The Sign

my mother at the window
watched to make sure
my walk home from school was safe

at the window she watched
she said in case the polio came

she watched for signs to see
if I needed snow boots
a raincoat   a warm hat

at the window now
she watches me hold up
the sign nate and I made
mom   grandma   we love you
here's ~~a hug~~ two hugs

it's about the virus
we can't go inside the home
she can't come out
she has the dementia

she turns to the nurse
I think there's someone
out there she says
with some kind of sign

Three Mothers

the funeral director sat me down
while your wife he said I mean your ex-wife chooses
a suitable container for your son's
wilson but you call him willi's cremains
I wanted to ask you while you're alone
cause I really don't want to mess this up
and it's true I've never had this particular situation before
you know the seating   the words and the names
the program   the order of the service
and like who's supposed to get the ashes

he raised his pen in the air and asked me
for the record and I mean no offense
exactly how many mothers did willi have

three in all I said he had three mothers
his birth mother mary who gave him up
her senior year after christmas break
and marilyn the adopting mother
who raised him   held him for twenty-six years
and stepmom sue who loved him to pieces

the funeral director wrote down the names
you know I always thought we only got one mom
me too I said that's how it was for me
having three mothers he said that's special isn't it
willi was pretty lucky wasn't he
with that he closed the notebook and sat back

yeah he sure was   I guess you could say that

Cross-eyed

superintendent sutherland
demanded to meet with my family
wednesday night after supper
he smiled briefly at my parents
then focused squarely on me

and what exactly were you thinking
don't you realize you've sinned
against the trinity baptist church
and the entire eastman kodak company
he asked me why for the love of god
did I really want to make baby jesus cry

I had to admit I had made a split
second decision on my part
just as the superintendent was about to snap
our third grade sunday school
class graduation picture
to grin and cross my eyes

my parents were struck dumb
when he produced the perforated photo in evidence
your son has managed single-handedly
to ruin our 1956 church family album

tears welled in my mother's eyes
as she stared at the portrait
of her white-shirted bow-tied boy
surrounded by girls in easter pastel pinafores

mom started to speak
but broke out in a laugh
grabbed her stomach rocking
back and forth trying clearly
not to split a gut

my dad glanced at the photo and guffawed
that's hilarious he said and slapped my knee

superintendent sutherland stood up
when the laughter died down
I took a breath and apologized
I never intended to make baby jesus cry I said
my mother rose and suppressed another chuckle
as she showed him the door saying
I'm so sorry it won't happen again
goodnight

he left   she shut the front door
and turned to face me
winked and pulled her dentures out
tugged her ears up
and crossed her eyes

Ma Come Get Me (the Phone Slams)

*Frosh football players: You will be kind to your mother when using
this phone to ask for a ride home. This is not a suggestion.*

fed up with players' rude phone calls
to their folks to pick them up after practice
as coach I scotch taped the following mandatory script
next to the phone in the coaching office
on august fifteenth nineteen eighty-one

players please dial your number carefully
assume a pleasant demeanor
say hello mom dad or name of guardian
and pause for response
say this is your son or daughter your name here
say I'm done with football practice
ask would you please come pick me up at the high school
and pause for response
say thank you very much
say I love you mom dad or name of guardian
and/or say goodbye
please hang the phone up gently

they could grumble that the coach made them
but every player always chose I love you

Renewable

I was real new I remember
come awfully early to the dance
my right ear rubbed across her housedress belly
right arm barely reached around her hip

okay my mother really was an okie
she sounded out a word she didn't know
and made up tunes to kitchen dance
that's how the word renewable
became the ree nee wobble song

she sang the word in warbled twang
we stepped stepped hopped then stepped

reeneewobble reeneewobble
down the cobbled street
reeneewobble reeneewobble
rosebuds for our feet

we made blue rosebud bottles clink
across the pantry shelves   I limped along
the knives and forks were sizzling in the drawer

was it rumi said god likes us when we sing
but loves us when we dance

we stepped stepped glistening sweaty
then hopped stepped laughing dropped

oh to pop open a rosebud bottle
rewind one more linoleum sundown
and redo mom's reeneewobble kitchen dance

Easter Parade 1953

when richard nixon was vice-president
and the philadelphia athletics decided to move to kansas city
old miss mintz my kindergarten teacher
organized another mother's spring tea
the boys made fedoras   the girls bonnets
from construction paper and le page glue
the girls made ribbons   the boys built bowties
barbara shoppe (sherry shoppe's little sister)
couldn't wait and glued her hat to her hair
she was forced to spend the rest of the day
locked in the bathroom "as an example"
an example of what I never knew
then we practiced our formal promenade
each couple strolling down fifth avenue
prancing around the classroom cakewalking
fashion plates in our own easter parade

miss mintz scrinched her leathery lips then said
something's missing   this just doesn't seem right
she turned to me with her hand on her chin
stroking the several long hairs on her chin
bruce, you know the words to easter parade
she chose me to sing for the mother's tea
practice at home but don't tell your mother
yes ma'am I said cause I was five years old
you do what your teacher tells you to do
I practiced secretly in my bedroom

on good friday we served moms cake and tea

the children put on their hats and fancies
I stood and sang   my classmates sashaying
I sang in my clear and falsetto voice
in your easter bonnet with all the frills upon it
I'll be the proudest fella in the easter parade

I saw her out the corner of my eye
my mom dropped her fork and grabbed her napkin
I noticed the tears streaming down her cheeks
I thought how sweet   what a good son I am
I finished the song and everyone clapped
I felt balloony and walked my mom home

years later after my son had been born
mom and I were looking at old photos
and there I was singing easter parade
mom I'm so sorry I brought you to tears
that's when I learned that tears weren't always sad

you're wrong mom said I was laughing so hard
I thought I would spit out my chocolate cake
and grabbed my napkin to cover my face
I laughed so bad I thought I'd pee myself

A Comedy of Onions

I start the onions frying
then go to watch tv
carol burnett tugs her ear
the smell of far off onions
jackie gleason glides how sweet it is
the smell of onions caramelizing
red skelton smiles may god bless
the smell of onions burning
mom hollers
you can't cook in the front room
funny how they can make you cry

The Child and the Mother

(for John)

she isn't feeling well at all
it's time to plump her pillow
tuck her in
brush her hair back
hold her hand
tell her you love her
kiss her cheek
keep the little light on for a while
hum her song and watch her sleep

how swift the nighthawk
flies above the hospice

where we come from

Where We Come From

when we asked where we come from
our sunday school teacher glen bodie
told us that if two people
really love each other
and they get down together
on their knees to pray extra hard
sometimes they get a baby

so for the longest time
after my little brother was born
I checked out my mother's knees
for signs of wear and tear
or worried when she complained
her knees for some reason were sore

excuse me but I know you'll understand
I'd rather not think about this
anymore

Roy Rogers Pocket Knife

aunt meave told me
if I ever give cutlery
to someone as a gift
you have to tape a penny
on the blade to ensure
love and friendship
will never be severed

it had something to do she said
with the mysterious elemental
power of copper
it also serves as hush money
a sort of prepaid apology
suggesting don't blame me
when you cut your dern finger off

my first knife
an authentic roy rogers single blade pocket knife
given to me on my sixth birthday
by my cousin ted
who didn't have the sense
god gave a goose
it was taped with a penny

when I was alone
I opened the blade
by the fingernail slot
and of course looked
for something to cut

much in the way hammers seek nails
and any surgeon worth her scalpel
says sure we can
take care of that for you

I remember whittling a stick
into a stake to put under my pillow
to fend off nocturnal
trellis climbing vampires
to demonstrate my newfound manly courage
I tossed the knife into the dirt
as close as I could come to my bare foot
my first attempt at mumbley-peg
it stuck between my toes way too close
at least it missed the meat thank goodness

I looked this way and that
the sweat cold on my forehead
I hurried and carelessly closed the knife
and somehow guillotined my pinky

my blood filled the little trough
where the blade should be seated
and oh my god I thought
I've cut my dern finger off

I ran cool water on my hand
at the bathroom sink
dried it on a white towel
and fumbled a bandaid tight

the blood dangling from my finger smelled like copper
the knife smelled like copper
my bedroom reeked
with the metallic tang of copper

roy and my knife sat hidden
in my top drawer for over a year
while I dreamed of trigger
and dancing puppets on strings
with pennies where their eyes should have been

I dreamed of love unsevered
and happy trails
rocking slowly in the saddle
on my sleeping pony

Open Mic

no the stars won't shine brighter
just because you had the guts
this time to get up and read your poem
but now you know you know
those stars are really really up there

careful working
on the farm
it's hard to hug
with just
one arm

burma-shave

a tattoo
of her boyfriend's smile
upon her breast did place
and after fifty years or so
he had the longest face

burma-shave

Safety Glass

mrs miller's class of first graders
had been good for a change and earned
a rare and extra ten-minute recess
we lined up like the teeth on a pocket comb
though crew cuts and ponytails don't beg combing
we ran outside to the tar hot playground
girls to the bricktop for jump rope
boys to the blacktop painted diamond
and realized we forgot the kickball
now there were less than ten minutes left

I hollered to ricky   run back in and get the ball
and hurry up   hurry back

I heard his red ball jets squeak on the steps
and saw the windowed school door close behind him
the clock ticked slowly
I ran to check his progress
kansas city gets hot in may
my missouri side sways with heat

ten minutes became nine
did I mention john j pershing elementary school
jaysus larry and joseph   ricky step on it

I heard the klank kapow just then
the door and the safety glass window exploded
ricky had stumbled down the steps to the door
in his haste to the playground

carrying the kickball   he missed the push bar
and slammed his arm through the glass

dust be diamonds wood be wine
happy happy happy
all the time time time

the meat from his right forearm dangled from his wrist
odd how human fat resembles sturgeon roe when opened
how wide can a person open his eyes

to this day I haven't found him to apologize
ou sont les nieges d'anton

the principal   the janitor   mrs miller
the bloody ice cubes of glass
the siren   the ambulance   the stretcher

ricky waved to me with his left hand
the kickball still under his arm
that ball always pacman in my dreams

mea culpa mea culpa felix culpa
it was my fault   I made him hurry
his blood now my blood
me   responsible for the attack on pearl harbor
the crucifixion
me   widowmaker the bucking bronco
in the playground rodeo

our ten minutes were up
recess was over   deserved or not
I knew I would never go to vietnam
and I make sure I always separate
every piece of the jigsaw puzzle
before I put it back in the box

Another Fine Transvaginal Mesh

it's child's play
way too easy to make some thoughtless offensive joke
about how now scientists can grow new nostril and vaginal tissue
and how boy I hope they don't get the tissues mixed up
because you know just one sneeze . . .

too easy like beating up harvey flax's sister
after she clonked me on the head with that baseball bat
just because I must have said something really stupid

or how thoughtlessly I laughed
when lorraine metcalf came running
into our sixth grade classroom from the girl's bathroom
screaming holy crap my ass is bleeding
and how ashamed I was later
so ashamed I would never tell anybody
especially you

and yes I'm very sorry for what I did
and no mom for the fifth time
I don't know what I was thinking
and I'm eleven years old
and of course I should have known better
and now I'll go to my room
to think hard about what I did for the next sixty-one years
if that's okay with you

Rachel's Face

it's the childish laugh
and that smile in her eyes
no mask can cover

Fabric

remember that baby you're having
you will build her a blanket
and you will choose the fabric
the warp and the weft of it
the weave and oh-so familiar feel
of the blanket you will wrap her in

select say fringe or satin edging
perhaps some blend of wool to scratch her nose
or cobble a quilt of yesterdays
tied off with yarns and knotted
depicting your strong ancestral women
lots of smart rabbits stars and moons
blocks of pine trees and storybooks

you will capture the color of rain from mountain clouds
the sunset lake   a sheet of frost
the crosshatch of each song you sing

it will smell so much like you
of baking bread   of night night kisses
of grandpa's blue bandana and august bicycle chains

and our little citizen will come to know your face
and the place she'll always call home

and when your child's child arrives
she'll navigate with careful fabrication
the blanket she will pass along

Company

there's this hotel in seattle that'll
send up a goldfish in a glass fishbowl
if you're a guest confessing loneliness
the only thing is you have to feed it
and name it something good and meaningful
sorry *goldie* and *russell wilson* are
already taken   so's *boeing boeing*

consider calling him *heart on my sleeve*
what a loser I am is a nice name
or *woe betide* or *my little pity*
hey you can always choose *goodbye cruel world*
or *nobody really understands me*

feed him   turn off the tv for a while
commit to spending some quality time
just you guys swimming in the goldfish bowl
remember there are two sides to the glass
and you could really use the company

when you're done with your work in seattle
and when you're packed up and ready to fly
back home to kansas city by yourself
say goodbye to *misery* and mean it
leave him swimming upright in his fishbowl
on the checkout counter at the front desk

Uninvited Guests

melon sellers in tegucigalpa
hang clear plastic bags of water on strings
above their fruit to scare the flies away
everyone knows a fly will see its own
reflection and buzz away in terror

I ask about buying a flyswatter
while I train honduran librarians
you don't need a matamoscas they say
get a cheap electric fan for your room
and when you are outside sit in the sun
the flies never come into libraries
why would they they never learned how to read

I see the starving child in darfur
too far gone to brush the flies from her eyes

back home I eat sel roti on the deck
with my nepali buddhist friend diwas
smack the living crap out of mosquitoes
and swat every fly that circles my plate
I am siva the destroyer when it
comes to dispatching uninvited guests

I see a fly land on diwas's wrist
slowly he raises his hand to his lips
blows the fly away with a puff of air
so naturally and goes back to his food

we eat and we talk we do what we're taught

I'm afraid I say the flies at this rate
will easily outnumber us some day
he unfolds his napkin and puts down his fork
so what exactly is your point he asks

Friendly Letter

dear jimmy
how are you   I am fine
I hope his letter finds you
mess with my sister betty one more time
and I will hit you so hard in the chest
that you and your whole family will die
yours truly
bruce
ps   how about those packers

Writing Tip #23

getting even one or two letters wrong
can change the entire erection of your poem
and can be as exasperating to remodel
as prying old broads off your porch for sex hours

Girls in Cars 1958

girls in cars
they blow me away
they make me crazy
they drive me insane

one year from now
I'll be attending junior high school
my hope's by then
they'll think I'm cool

once one of them waved
I could smell their hair and stuff when they went past
I'm sure I could save enough
money to help pay for gas

corvette stingrays
edsel tanktop station wagons packed with girls
or buick coupes
convertible curls

girls in cars
girls in cars
mmmgirls in cars
(ouch) girls in cars

someday I pray
maybe they'll ask me to come ride around
until that day
they're all I dream about

girls in cars
they blow me away
they make me mmmcrazy crazy
they drive me insane

Preservation Prayer

god grant me the saran wrap
to preserve the food I cannot can
the shelf space for what I can can
and the wisdom to assign
some kind of expiration date
or so

Cutting Chickens

I got off the prospect bus at eighteenth street
on the already scorching morning of june fifteenth 1963
walked one steamy block east to montgall market
my dad and uncle's grocery store
to cut whole chickens into fryer pieces
so hot I thought at this rate kansas city
would catch fire by three o'clock

I carried the forty pound waxed cardboard box
filled with chickens and ice from the walk-in cooler
uncle russell said careful the knives are sharp this morning
cold meat is the coldest thing to handle
the pain shoots up between your shoulder blades

I cut the wings off first
then slice between the breast and thigh to remove the legs
fish out the paper bag of heart gizzard neck and liver
saw deep to separate the breast from the back
uncle russell says kansas city folks like themselves
some big breasts and shoots me a wink
I hack the back in two
and lance then pop the sternum out to divide the breast
the pieces are arranged just so in the paper tray
the backs and innards on the bottom
frame the two legs at the corners
fold the wings into triangles to fit
and cover with the breasts
each pack is wrapped in clear plastic and weighed
priced and displayed in the meat case

the green aisles of parsley
make the meat look redder fresher

one box done I lingered in the cooler
as I wiped the sweat from my face
I read the front page headline
on wednesday's folded kansas city star
just after midnight medgar evers had been gunned down
in his driveway in jackson mississippi
the rifle bullet entered his back
and tore his chest away
his wife and children stuffed a mattress into the station wagon
he died on the way to the hospital
by custom he would have an open casket

half the kids in my high school freshman class were black
I hoped they hadn't seen the paper

when I was four brother calvin preached
that we as christians we're bound to help the needy
red and yellow black and white
they are precious in his sight

my grandfather used a different word
that started with n for these folks
mostly customers at our store
I must have blended the words
and when I called them the neegie people
the grownups would laugh

I cut up another box of chickens
and caught the bus back home

I ate popcorn that night
and suffered this burning feeling in my hands
uncle russell's knives were too sharp
so sharp the nicks and incisions hadn't even bled
the pain rose red from beneath my skin
from the salt in the wounds

time in time out

Red Granite Correctional C Block

the new prisoner's name is 6014293 his new
forest green pants and shirt have no pockets
his new white tennis shoes will never get dirty
his new watch and radio are transparent plastic
and the new stamp on the letter he writes
to his children tonight says forever

Time In Time Out

you walk in and show your ID
you sign the book   time in 5:37 pm
you pick up your badge
drop your quarter and put your wallet
your watch your keys and phone in the locker
you place your notebook and pencils
your belt and shoes and coat in the x-ray tub
walk through the metal detector
reclaim your belt and shoes and coat
your notebook and your pen
they stamp the back of your hand
you wait till the door buzzes and clicks open
you walk
you wait till the first gate buzzes and clicks
you walk
you wait till the second gate buzzes and clicks
you walk fifty yards under the umbrellas of razor wire
past the towers the shadows to enter the classroom block
you stop and hold your hand under the black light
you go in sit down
and wait for the dozen men in forest green to arrive
you give the first writing prompt   my gift
you wait ten minutes and one man comes to the microphone
my gift he says and wipes his face then reads
the wife called yesterday
she said our baby walked
my baby said I walk daddy I walk
that's good baby that's real good   he pauses
this was my gift he says and sits down

and when class is over
I say goodbye to the men who live there
then walk through the first gate
walk through the second gate the door
I hear the buzzers and the metal clicking tight
hold my hand under the black light
take my badge off
cross my name off   time out 8:17 pm
get my things from the locker
put the quarter back in my pocket
and walk out
I put my coat on
and I walk out

Reminding

the immense inmate looks down on me
you dye your hair man

no I don't

your beard's all white and shit
your hair's all brown
you dye your hair man

no I really don't

I'm tellin' you
you dye
your hair
man

I look up
yes you're right
thanks for reminding me

I dye my hair

Playing the Blues at the Tomah VA

tell me what I need   I need to know you
show me how they held you when you fell
tell me how they chose the name they named you
chased away those demons for a spell

how do you dance when no one is around
pound your wheelchair twice if you can hear me
did you cross your buddy's red red river
do the dreamers warn you when you're near me

if I pull the string between your shoulders
will you share the deepest secret that you keep
the one where spiders swim in vats of honey
and white-faced clowns surround you as you sleep

tell me what I need I need to know you
slowly as your fingers twirl your tired hair
tap the wheelchair armrest if you hear me
to show me if you know I'm here or there

Fox Lake Correctional Chapel August 2012

three floor fans
one cross
one star of david
one crescent
one feather
one guard
the next writing prompt
is tick tock
you have ten minutes
go
twenty-four pencils
twenty-four sheets of paper
twenty-four poets
in forest green uniforms

Prison Poem Prompt

I choose this writing prompt
for these men who live in prison
ten men in forest green
whose boots are always clean

write a message to your younger self
think about some advice maybe
some helpful information to pass along
and at the end add a feeling or emotion line
or a warning maybe   be specific

they write with yellow pencils without erasers
some men fidget or tap their toes
as they scratch on their clipboards
a few men stare at the floor
one man he's crying

ready I say   who wants to start
ed I'll call him ed   bald headed
murderously tattooed   black eyed
walks to the podium and begins to read aloud

boy you need to learn how to forgive
you don't deserve this life
the beatings will not last forever
there are safe ways to end arguments
other people have feelings
know you're not alone
I love you   I love everything about you

oh yeah heads up about diane
at the pussy palace in reno in 1992
chick's a dude

without you

Sometimes

sometimes at readings I read poems
about the death of my son
a motorcycle spill near waunakee
the grief of it   the skid marks
the evaporated futures

and sometimes afterwards
women mostly mothers
approach me with tears in their eyes
they say I'm sorry for your loss
my son died too
he took his own life

and sometimes
they open their arms for permission
and give me a hug

and sometimes
they take a slow breath
and ask me
was it my fault?

and sometimes I cry
sometimes right away
sometimes later

but I always say
and I always mean it
no it wasn't your fault
never

Without You

so this is what
the world looks like
without you
the trees still grow
the winds still blow
the sky's on top
the ground's below
my empty heart
fills up with nothing
and this is how
the world looks like
without you

My Take

she took my hands in hers
and made her saddest face
she told me how how sorry she was
to have my son taken from me that way
god she said he must have needed
another angel in heaven

I took a breath   I took my hands away
I could have said
oh thank you for your heartfelt words
your kind and sympathy
your depth of understanding
hey your what you call it empathy

I could have said
yes he's in a better place
I could have said
please take this bitter cup from me

I could have said
jesus christ lady
don't you think god could have made
another angel if she wanted to
I mean what would it take   just one wave of her hand
would it have killed her   really

I could have said
well nothing   so that's what I said   nothing
and took my leave from her

next I took the hand of an old man I didn't know
he hugged me and whispered in my ear   tough luck
yes I said

so that's my take on all of this
get in line   say whatever you need to say
but don't you ever take my grief away from me

The Belonging Song

(for Ellen Kort)

choose the longest leg bone of the poet
place the bone in the clearing on the stump
wet it with your tears   bleach it in the sun
for years let mice chew an octave of holes
the wind will whistle through its hollowness
wind from the west makes the saddest music
the east wind plays the laughter of children
hide the bone inside the pocket closest
to your heart   feel it vibrate hum and sing
the oldest songs   the song of acceptance
tune of inclusion   song of belonging
there is no metaphor   the poet's bone
tells you forever you're no place but home
you're no place but home   you're no place but home

Visitors

(are people you see for a while then don't)

you told me every sound ever made's still
encapsulated in earth's atmosphere
and if we only had the right device
we could listen to the dinosaur's roar
or mark anthony's farewell to caesar

yes that's the cry you made when you were born
the song you wrote for your bongzilla band
you asked me what I thought the answers were
and why your mother and I got divorced
how the pine branches scrape the rising moon
what's an absentee landlord or father
how to keep a ukulele in tune
and is there a chance I could visit soon

Wife

my wife died last october
my second wife
my ex-wife
she got her diagnosis
she stopped her doctoring and died

we were married some sixteen years
it seemed like a lifetime
I remember her throaty laugh
her melody voice and crooked smile
I don't remember the fights
her tears my tears
after a while we learned to get along

no funeral   no ceremony
and now she's gone

sometimes you turn left
sometimes you turn right
and sometimes you turn left again

I'll Be Leaving Then

just a quick note
pork chops and summer squash are in the fridge next to the soymilk
let keeper out twice a day
remember only two cups of dog food
once in the morning and once when you get home
please empty the dryer
don't forget the birthday card for your mom
pick up your prescriptions at the pharmacy
put my mail on the dining room table
call fred about replacing the windows
the extra lightbulbs are in the basement
don't get too upset about the packers (they're doing their best)
eddie next door will keep the grass mowed
talk to him about shoveling the driveway later on
it wouldn't kill you to vacuum once in a while
and floss your teeth (I'm serious)
choose your medicare supplement and renew your library card
learn a couple new jokes and memorize a poem or two
you never know when you'll be stuck in an elevator
vote regularly and speak your peace
remember music and dance make us human (don't let anybody tell
you different)
spoil any grandkids that come along
ban all handguns and automatic weapons
realize then vocalize when you need to ask for help
stop the wars in iraq afghanistan syria and north korea
preserve clean air and clean water
find out who killed kennedy
honk if you find jesus (I didn't know he was missing ha ha)

and avoid any nuclear holocausts (you know what happened last
time)
what am I forgetting
oh yeah save the refugees
colonize mars if possible
and try to keep us in one piece until the federation comes
so I'll be leaving then
take good care of yourself
goodbye

Note to Self

bread
milk
lettuce

plastic sheet
smith & wesson
bullet(s)

mortgage
cell phone
water bill

letter to sheryl
mom and dad
brothers

video for junior
missy
woofer

insurance guy
pastor
change of address form

Touched by an Angler

I will make you fishers of men.
--Jesus of Nazareth

fully half of all the fishermen
found drowned
are fished out
with their zippers down

it seems a little overboard
these poor capsized baptized
miscalculating urinating
anglers   their fate upended
soups de jerque

and makes me speculate
about which bait
they had intended
using as a lure

Calling

this dying shit's a bitch

at eight thirty this morning
my boom voice tango poet friend died
how many times at readings when somebody
went on and on about why they wrote
the poem and what the poem means
he'd holler from the back of the room
just read the damn poem

at twelve thirty my brother-
in-law the teacher the harmonica
playing world conservator died
he always said there's a fine line
between numerator and denominator
and only a fraction of the population
would come to understand this concept fully

you others please
I want you to take your phone
and call your mother your father
your son your daughter
an old friend maybe
I want you to tell them you love them
and ask them to call someone they love
it's okay   come on   I'll wait
I have all the time in the world
there you go I'm waiting
all done?   good

did you hear them smile?
did you feel the sizzle?

hang on a second   get ready
now I'm going to call you

Tango

(for Richard Roe)

yo tango contigo
embrace me   turn   step   slide
your eyes   your eyes
twirl   dip   entwine
your touch   the scent of you
no smile   the business of tango is serious
beguiled   that tingle of hesitation
llorando sin lagrimas
the crying with no tears

fantasma mio   bailez conmigo
hear the saddest violin   bandoneon
the terror in the rise and fall of us
so dreadfully entangled
leave me   do not leave me
take me
make me tango contigo

Maybe Wednesday

my boy rode a moped
and failed to negotiate a left turn
north of lake mendota

he made no attempt to catch himself
as he spilled and hit his head on the pavement
no helmet
it was sunny and maybe wednesday

the next day the rain washed the pavement
the sun came out as it rained
and I hoped to catch a rainbow
as I sat there and waited by the road
but there was no rainbow to speak of

it's okay I'll wait for one

so I sat there by the road
rocking back and forth
and waited and waited some more

Losing Purchase

my boots lose purchase
as I make my way down the frozen path to little lake
where eight years ago
I stopped to cry when my other son died

in early march little lake thaws during daytime and freezes at night
crusty oak leaves cling to shaky branches
soon pushed out and fall when spring buds bloom
I have to walk beside the icy path to gain foothold
funny how the darkened leaves
melt these perfect impressions sunk in the road

two geese honk to warn me to stay away
but I make myself walk out to the middle of the lake
mindful not to slip and break the ice
I understand I could crash through
submerge and gasp to stay afloat and gulp for air
in broken ice splinters and spray
swirling downward deeply down
and still I think oh what a beautiful day
though this might be my last on earth alive

I decide to return to shore
there are two sides to the ice
one upside and one down
one bright and sunny warm
one dark and most coldblooded
funny how there are people here you love
and then there aren't

how someone is
and then he's not

I make sure my boots are under me
gain purchase and walk carefully
back to the dock   this time

I think about my son my sons
I see his face their faces
I say his name their names
I hug the wooden rail
and cry goodbye goodbye

March 3, 2018

better get used to it
I have no more sons to give you
and death you selfish bastard
I've survived to live another spring
winter your days are numbered
in the leafless crabapple tree
I see my first robin
in the leafless crabapple tree
winter your days are numbered
I've survived to live another spring
and death you selfish bastard
I have no more sons to give you
better get used to it

Wind Chimes

on the night before valentine's day
we were walking home in the snow
from bentley's pharmacy
you look rose said
like you just stepped out
of a goodwill basement catalog

I hadn't planned to be seen in public
and I didn't think
goodwill even had a catalog

we'd bought valentine cards
to send to our family and friends
in sarasota and green bay

we noticed the sign outside the methodist church
chili supper   all the fixins and pie 4:30 to 7:00 pm
and decided why not
we wouldn't have to cook
we wouldn't have to do the dishes

we entered the church
and stomped the snow off our boots
nothing else in the world
smells like church basement coffee

rose looked at me
and repeated the goodwill catalog crack
okay   I was wearing a green and gold packer's stocking cap
a brown and orange plaid scarf and a blue jacket
a purple sweatshirt from the wisconsin
fellowship of poets that read
poetry is life   life is poetry

I pocketed the stocking cap
and the scarf and smoothed back my hair
there that's better she said

we paid bonnie and got our chili bowls
we chose chili with noodles or not
green tabasco sauce and grated cheese
and picked out our pie

we sat with bev and judy and dixie
who all grew up on farms
near mount morris and coloma
we talked about bad lettuce
the fatal school bus accident
some virus in china
and when are they going to have
some good news on tv for a change

the chili warmed us
I drank my see-through coffee
and ate a big slice of homemade
dutch apple pie with cool whip

we said goodbye and walked in the snow
in the cold early dark
as we got close to home the wind came up
and rang the wind chimes
a gift from the office women
to remind us of our son
who died exactly two years before
on february thirteenth

we knocked the snow off our boots
and went into the house
rose wrote notes on the valentines
and I addressed and stamped the envelopes
she fell asleep in the chair until bedtime

they're a little late I thought
but I'll mail them in the morning

it's never too late
to tell them you love
you love them

Papá's Lullaby

separation at the border

pobrecito   niño mío
you're alone and the night is so long
it's the reason I give you this song
you must be strong

hear the music from abuela's garden
there is nothing can keep us apart
know your papá he loves you
and holds you deep in his heart

pobrecito   you can sleep now
close your eyes   here's a kiss maybe two
no importa whatever they do
I am with you

hear the music from abuela's garden
there is nothing can keep us apart
know your papá he loves you
and holds you deep in his heart

when your sandals are under the bed
hug your pillow and lay down your head

Sun Black

I tried to read his favorite
poem at my son his fun
his fune   read at his funeral
~~he d~~ you see he died there was
a motorcycle a sunny black motorcycle
and red the blood his head was
red on one side and the asphalt
was black and hot and sundown red
at my son his funeral
and the yellow helicopter and the helpers
fred said   fred rogers said the helpers
fred mcfeely rogers said
~~look~~ you can be sad or you can
look at all the helpers   oh
mister rogers help me ~~the~~ read the

About the Author

Bruce Dethlefsen was born in Kansas City, Missouri in 1948 and moved to Wisconsin in 1966. He was Wisconsin Poet Laureate (2011-2012). A retired school librarian and public library director, he plays in the Prairie Sands Band and runs poetry workshops in Wisconsin prisons. *Losing Purchase* is his fourth full-length book of poems.

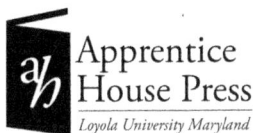

**Apprentice
House Press**
Loyola University Maryland

Apprentice House is the country's only campus-based, student-staffed book publishing company. Directed by professors and industry professionals, it is a nonprofit activity of the Communication Department at Loyola University Maryland.

Using state-of-the-art technology and an experiential learning model of education, Apprentice House publishes books in untraditional ways. This dual responsibility as publishers and educators creates an unprecedented collaborative environment among faculty and students, while teaching tomorrow's editors, designers, and marketers.

Eclectic and provocative, Apprentice House titles intend to entertain as well as spark dialogue on a variety of topics. Financial contributions to sustain the press's work are welcomed. Contributions are tax deductible to the fullest extent allowed by the IRS.

To learn more about Apprentice House books or to obtain submission guidelines, please visit www.apprenticehouse.com.

Apprentice House
Communication Department
Loyola University Maryland
4501 N. Charles Street
Baltimore, MD 21210
Ph: 410-617-5265
info@apprenticehouse.com • www.apprenticehouse.com